Anonymous

The message of the world's religions

Anonymous

The message of the world's religions

ISBN/EAN: 9783337263768

Printed in Europe, USA, Canada, Australia, Japan

Cover: Foto ©Lupo / pixelio.de

More available books at **www.hansebooks.com**

THE MESSAGE
OF THE
WORLD'S RELIGIONS

THE MESSAGE

OF THE

WORLD'S RELIGIONS

REPRINTED FROM "THE OUTLOOK"

NEW YORK
LONGMANS, GREEN, AND CO.
LONDON AND BOMBAY
1898

COPYRIGHT, 1897, BY
THE OUTLOOK COMPANY

COPYRIGHT, 1898, BY
LONGMANS, GREEN, AND CO.

All rights reserved

Press of J. J. Little & Co.
Astor Place, New York

CONTENTS

JUDAISM 1
    By Rabbi Gustav Gottheil, D.D.

BUDDHISM 23
    By Professor T. W. Rhys Davids, Ph.D., LL.D.

CONFUCIANISM 41
    By the Rev. Arthur H. Smith
        Author of "Chinese Characteristics"

MOHAMMEDANISM 65
    By the Rev. George Washburn, D.D.
        President of Robert College, Constantinople

BRAHMANISM 86
    By Charles R. Lanman
        Professor of Sanskrit in Harvard University

CHRISTIANITY 102
    By Lyman Abbott, D.D.

THE MESSAGE OF THE WORLD'S RELIGIONS

I

JUDAISM

By Rabbi Gustav Gottheil, D.D.

The perseverance of the Jew and his Judaism is in itself a mission to the world. That it is the wonder of history is generally allowed; but why should a wonder be wrought, if not to teach and enforce a lesson? Goethe looked upon it in that light; for he wrote: "In regard to independence, firmness, courage—and where these qualities do not suffice, tenacity—the people of Israel is without compare. It is the most enduring race on earth, *which was, is, or shall be*, that it may glorify the name of Jehovah forever. It is for this reason that (in the pictorial representation of history which meets the eye of the son of Meister in the Octagon hall) we have placed Israel as the great ensample and central picture which the others surround as a frame merely." The wonder is justified in our eyes when we remember that his "tenacity" is the very sin which the Church cannot forgive. She has done all she can, and much more than she ever ought to have done, to make the wonder cease; but " the arm of the Lord is not shortened to save." Officially she has not changed her attitude toward Israel; she continues to place his mission against the mission of God; but silently, and in the hearts of her most thoughtful sons and daughters, the question has sprung up, and is pressing for an answer more urgently day by day: How was it possible for these scattered remnants, numerically so weak, and that small number broken up and scattered to the four winds, to "stand and to withstand" for so many centuries? To stand, with every known support of a nation struck away; with every national bond rent asunder; without an organization of any kind, without a priesthood, without a rallying-point or outward symbol of unity, national or spiritual? Here are ten millions of people, strewn over vast areas of lands, with whole continents and oceans between the "disjecta membra," yet owning an affinity that has never been found wanting in the hour of need. This wonder has been so exasperating to the enemies of Israel that they invented all sorts of devilish plots to account for it; plots that have now been brooded over by the clumsy emissaries of Satan for centuries, but never were consummated yet. Meanwhile these mysterious men and women have lived their honest lives and have passed away like other sons and daughters of Adam, have inscribed names on the roll of benefactors that yield to none in lustre, and not a few of them have given their lives in the defence of the country which they called their own. How could a race, so situated and conditioned, "withstand" the ceaseless and merciless war made upon it for so long a time? Needs not that I open that register once more—it is sufficiently known. True, their disruption was their building up, wherein we see the hand of Providence working its own ends irresistibly: fractions only could be destroyed, or, if exiled, find a refuge somewhere on earth; the rare instances in which brethren refused to open their doors to the fugitives or even showed selfish coldness are branded in Jewish records with an indelible mark of infamy. This was in cases of open war; but open war was not the hardest test of Jewish tenacity and courage; to be slain not the worst of fates; for the martyr's crown cast a halo around the darkness of the grave. To live, aye! to live under the most refined wickedness of persecution was more bitter than death—was, did I say? Is, to this hour. Very recently one who knows what he is testifying to, and may be fully trusted, said to me: "Sir, the distress, the poverty, the want to which the Jews encaged in the Russian Pale have been reduced is appalling; it is beyond my power of description; and there is but one cry sounding from all letters received: 'For God's sake take us anywhere you can, so that we have enough to eat and to drink.'" But where such distress does not exist, nay, even where plenty reigns and the political rights of the Jew are not questioned, his race and his religion are the gall and wormwood in the cup of the Jew. Without doubt, whether we consider the length of time, or the severity of the trial, or the absence of friend and comforter, no other faith has been tried as has that of Israel. Others have had their periods of persecution and oppression, but they were followed by triumph and dominion; others have covered the pages of history with martyrs and professors who proved invincible under their tortures, and who went to the stake singing psalms and giving praise to God that they were found worthy to seal the truth with their blood; who better than the Jew can honor their memory? But, with the exception of two or three interruptions, the way of the Jew has been a "Via Dolorosa" from the thirteenth to the nineteenth century; and, in the words of his own inimitable elegist, he can say, "Behold, is there a grief like mine?"

All this would be wonderful, even if Jew and Judaism were now in their dotage; if their energy were spent, and they were listless as to the present, aimless as to the future; if Byron's word were true:

<blockquote>Israel has the grave.</blockquote>

But the outcry against the Jew is that his strength is far in excess of his number, that his ambition reaches to heights to which he is not entitled; his successes are the despair of his non-Jewish competitors. And as regards his religion, it is safe to say that it is, at the present day, the most active and energetic in the work of reform. The oldest of churches offers the heartiest welcome to the latest born of ideals. Nor is it a mere negative reform which is pursued; I mean, one that is content with the lopping of dead branches and the leaving undone of things that have fallen out of joint with the time. Young branches are being constantly grafted on the old stem which is found to be still full of sap, capable to nourish and prosper the fresh shoots. Old liturgies are expurgated and new ones composed; rituals and ceremonials are being modernized; new hymns written, or borrowed from other churches without compunction—sometimes even with their melodies, if text and tone appear to be made for each other; even new days and seasons are fixed for public worship. In schools, seminaries, periodicals, religious literature, societies, charities—everywhere the breath of a new life is felt. And, more astonishing still, the soil of Palestine is being reclaimed by the hands of Jewish peasants and planters; Jerusalem lifts her head once more and begins to lay aside her sackcloth and ashes—growing rapidly into a modern city.

And—here the superlative of wonder fails me—next August, in this year eighteen hundred and ninety-seven, a congress of Jews from all parts of the world will meet at Munich, Bavaria, to discuss the whole of the Jewish question and the most effective way of settling it; and also the question whether the founding of a Jewish State in Palestine is possible—if possible, desirable—as a refuge for those Jews who are not permitted by the people among whom they live to assimilate with them in citizenship.

Brief and summary as I desire to make this statement of the case, I cannot omit the fact that Judaism gave birth to two giant children, which cast their mother so far into the shade as regards numbers, power, wealth, brilliance, organization, and recognition in the world; that she can hardly be mentioned by their side. Well-nigh half of mankind live by a religious faith Jewish at the core, yet that great outpouring of her strength has not diminished her own store; the mother lives, and so far from preparing for her final exit, is girding up her loins to do and to dare yet more for humanity. She clings to her post as one of the pathfinders for the arrival of the Messiah, whose authority will rest on the fact that there will be no questioning, no wrangling about it, that all the earth will answer in unison, " Blessed be he that cometh in the name of the Lord."

And now I have been asked to offer an explanation of that wonder of history. I frankly confess that I have none to offer, neither have I met with one who could do it for me. After searching and sounding and probing and listening on all sides, I still must bow my head before the Power that lives and moves in this great mystery. Happy I, if I may humbly trace some of the means by which the miracle was wrought and is being continued. I do so with fear and trembling; more than once did I lay down the pen in the hopeless sense of my insufficiency; had I not feared that there was more cowardice than humility in this confession, I would never have pressed the pen back into the reluctant hand. I need both—the grace of God and the indulgence of the reader; and I ask for them in all sincerity and earnestness.

I.—UNITY

The taproot of Judaism is the idea of unity; the Rabbis understood this when they wrote on Israel's banner the words of their patriarch, the Deuteronomist, " Hear, O Israel: The Lord our God, the Lord is one." In unity there is strength of both faith and faithfulness. In the one and one only God the simplest mind and the profoundest thinker meet together. The singer of the shepherd psalm, that classical expression of childlike trust, says in song what Bruno and Spinoza say in their architectural systems. There is something grand and soul-subduing in that thought; and at the same time it allows a freedom of construction which keeps the soul in healthy activity and secures a sense of independence and self-esteem. One God or none at all—the alternative is bracing and stimulating. The issue is not that of the Jew, but of thinking man all over the world, and has been so from the time he began to reflect on the problem. The Jew feels that he has a place, indisputable and unavoidable, in the development of the human mind and the history of religion; that he is fully entitled to it, and in holding fast to it he defends the native right of humanity.

It has been said, and justly so, that it is the enemy that makes a nation. The pressure of defence and the dread of danger are needed to drive people together and to create a sense of unity. Now, by the proclamation of the vanity of all idols and of all ideas of Deity other than the one Israel proclaimed, he provoked the whole world to enmity; and in proportion to this enormous pressure from all sides grew his power of adhesion and resistance. He was and is right in allowing no tampering with his foundation faith, under whatever pretext. The term Monotheism he dislikes, because there lurks danger in it, as he sees clearly in the Trinitarian construction of that term in Christianity. His feet planted on his "Rock" (God is called by that name in his Bible), he watches with sleepless eye every attempt to undermine his foothold.

A Trinitarian belief is to him a disintegration of his clear and compact faith, and multiplies the arguments against God by three. It is the conception of unity, absolute, everlasting, unvarying, which alone can give us a perfect God; for this could not be with imperfections and limitations in His being. If such appear to our view, the fault must lie in our vision, not in Him.

And from this central idea a tendency towards unity went out like rays from the sun to pervade all Judaism. One people, the sons of Abraham, Isaac, and Jacob; one land, with one capital and one sanctuary, and in this one spot where the glory of God dwelt, visited by one man, once a year, on the unique fast-day of the year; one book, not the Bible, but the Law of Moses, the Torah, given through the prophet of whom it is written, There never arose another like him in Israel. One law for all, the stranger included, and—no monarchy; for a throne with a human being on it means division, not unity, as the very history of Israel proves better than any other national experience. Moses, incomparable fashioner of a nation and prince of legislators, wanted no dynasty; and those who followed in his footsteps, how true they remained to his great idea! From Joshua to Samuel—these were much-disturbed times, and many saviors of the nation arose, but no throne was established till the people themselves, in an evil hour, insisted on having one like other nations—and it was not long before the breach occurred that could never be healed again.

And so in the great outlook towards the consummation of Israel's oneness, the idea of unity, in heaven and on earth, if I may say so, appears triumphant at last. "In that day God will be one, and His name be one." Then God will burn the lip of nations and purify it that they shall all call upon the name of God and serve Him with one consent. Much more might be said on that point, but I must leave off here, and turn to what we must designate as the second great resource of Judaism; and that is:

II.—DIRECTNESS

Let the reader forbear criticism as to the name of this part of my statement; I chose *faute de mieux*, and will explain at once that Judaism places the soul in direct, immediate relation to the Creator. It offers no mediator, and hence has nothing corresponding to the Christian conception of "a Church." The

Jew must be his own bishop, his own pope. His Rabbi is no priest, and, with the exception of two or three instances in which a perfect knowledge of the law is absolutely required, there is no religious function which the Jew cannot perform legally and effectively for himself without the intercession of a Rabbi. Consistently with this religious democracy, the study of the Law, as expounded in the Talmud and the Casuists, is declared to be a universal duty; nay, one of the chief obligations of the Jew. And so you might see, if you thought it worth your while to see it, on any morning, winter or summer, hundreds of the "old-fashioned ones" leave their homes at four in the morning to go to the Beth-Hamidrash, or home of religious study, and spend the early hours of the day in that sacred pursuit, before they begin their wanderings or toilings to earn the pittances on which they and their families manage to live.

I do not underrate the enormous power which the idea of "a Church" as a divinely ordained institution is fitted to develop; a thought of what Catholicism has achieved is enough to convince us of that. But, at the same time, according to the law of compensation and adjustment of the balance, the Church must exact obedience and submission, and deprecate self-reliance, the free exercise of reason. Judaism demands the latter, and trusts its fate to it. Any ten male Jews past the age of thirteen may form a body, entitled to all the rights and immunities of a congregation, and perform public worship, wherever they may be and at whatever time they may desire it. Every synagogue is truly a people's church, and makes government not an easy matter by any means. The Rabbi is entirely thrown upon his own resources as regards weight and influence in the congregation. All attempts at ecclesiastical organization have so far failed among the Jewish ministry. It is not congenial to the spirit of Judaism; the merest approach to it is viewed with suspicion. Whether modern times and altered conditions and ideas will work a change in that respect remains to be seen. So far the grand principle of Rabbi Chananyah ben Teradyon prevails: where two sit together and interchange words of the Law, the Shekinah is between them; nay, even where one sits alone and devoutly gives his mind to the study of the Law, the Divine Presence is with him, and he receives his full reward.

III.—THIS-WORLDLINESS

That which strikes me as a third preservative element in the constitution of Judaism must seem strange in the eye of the reader, inasmuch as it is everywhere considered and treated as a reproach and a deficiency—I mean its *This-worldliness*. Strange enough that a religion which existed, and surely not idly, for a thousand years before the first faint mutterings of "another and a better world" are heard in its midst, should grow into the faith of martyrdom and outstrip all others in that regard! Yet so it is; and, what is more surprising still is that, despite the terrible denial which the Jew's experience gave to his belief that God's justice rewards obedience to His Law with earthly happiness and well-being, he held fast to it, and, as it were, assisted God to make good His promises given in His Word. Even after he received and approved the outlook into a "Hereafter," his faith in the "Here" suffered no diminution. It sometimes appears to me as if the Jew held it part of his mission to

> strive with might and main
> For worldly good and earthly gain

so as to vindicate the ways of his God to man; a mere fancy of mine, no doubt, but fancies are often only facts read in a peculiar way; and peculiar ways are not incongruous with a peculiar people!

However that may be, the truth remains the same: Judaism lays all stress upon religion as the wisest plan of spending this life well, and its kingdom of heaven meant a God's kingdom on earth, visible, tastable, measurable, calculable; thus remaining true to the conception of the Master of masters—the son of Amram, to whom cleanliness was godliness, and a healthful body the holiest temple of a soul created in the image of God. I cannot imagine him as frowning at a good joke; and so I will revive here one made by "Kladderadatsch" (the Berlin "Puck") when trichinæ were first discovered as revelling in swine's flesh; he said of Moses: "Das nenn' ich einen Geheimen Medizinal-Rath!"

So deeply rooted with the Jews was

the serious meaning of this life and what it offers or denies, at all times, that even to his hope of immortality he gave a this-world turn. His motto in this respect was the word: The memory of the just is for a blessing. His dead are not allowed to die for the memory. During the whole of the first year after death his ritual prescribes a prayer to be recited at the stated services by the mourners; and the anniversaries of deaths are loyally kept by children even if they live to a ripe old age.

When, therefore, the religious life of Europe in the beginning of this century began to take a turn towards the life that now is and the amelioration of its conditions, the Jews were among the readiest to receive and cultivate the new spirit. They looked upon it as a confirmation of the hope and the faith by which they have been sustained so long; and they are now found among the most active promoters of institutions designed to bring a little nearer the earthly paradise of which we have been dreaming and singing and preaching for so long a time.

Suppose we reach to it as near as this earth permits, will Judaism still survive, or be absorbed, voluntarily or otherwise, in the realization of its ideals? Who can tell! This only is certain: its merits will not pass out of the memory of men. Can we Jews be satisfied with this consummation? Why not! What is good for individual man must be good for any conglomeration of men; and what is better for the individual than the thought that the best fruit of his toil has nourished the best life of the world? That such a crown will some time be placed on the brow of Judah is certain. The rest is in God's hand.

II

BUDDHISM

By Professor T. W. Rhys Davids, Ph.D., LL.D.
Oxford University.

The future Buddha (the founder of the great system of religion and philosophy which we call Buddhism, and which he called the Dhamma or the Norm) was born in the sixth century B.C., in a noble family of Aryan descent, then settled at a place called Kapila-vatthu, near what is now the boundary between British India and Nepal. How, in his twenty-ninth year, he left his wife and only child and went out into the wilderness to become a homeless wanderer; how he spent six years of probationary studies into the mysteries of life; how, after much mental struggle, he at last deemed himself to have discovered the solution of that mystery, and came forward as a teacher of the new doctrine; how he founded the Buddhist Order, that oldest and most influential of all mendicant Orders; and how he died peacefully forty-five years afterwards, is now well known to all. What we have to consider for a short space are the salient features of that philosophy of life which he set forth.

When he began to think, it was not so much the fear of the gods that most filled with awe the minds of previous thinkers, as the fear of transmigration. The belief in the transmigration of souls, everywhere a part of primitive animism, had then acquired in the valley of the Ganges a power and a vitality much greater, much more influential, than it had at a similar stage in the religious evolution of other ancient peoples. Very real, very constantly present to the minds of ordinary men, the idea filled the heart of the more thoughtful with a vague dread of the future. How was this transmigration to end? Where, even after endless æons of different lives in different bodies, could the soul look to find rest and peace at last? Even a rebirth in heaven offered no security. For the gods and the angel-spirits, however long the duration of their bliss, were doomed to fall, in their turn, from their high estate, and be reborn, according to their deeds, in other bodies.

The most imaginative and poetic thought they had found a way of escape. They postulated a god, higher than all other gods, a personification of the mystic words of the ancient sacrifice, Brahmā, in whom all else that lived found its life. The logical conclusion was further drawn that all matter also was derived from Brahmā, was Brahmā. It is an error to trace back into pre-Buddhistic literature the notion of an absorption after death into this all-pervading deity. It was enough for the thinkers of that day that the man who, in this life, realized the identity of his own soul with Brahmā, would, when he died, go to the Brahmā world, and thence never return, never be reborn. Thus, and thus only, was a firm resting-place to be found. The peace realized already in this life as a consequence of the sense of identity with God would never pass away.

This theory, though common to various schools among the Brahmins, was confined to the few. It was taught, in poorest hermitages, as a mystery attainable only by the select, the deepest thinkers, and even by them only by the grace of God. The mass of the people, when they thought about such things, were content, as we see from the funeral ceremonies, to look forward to a rebirth among the departed fathers in the world of the gods. The more religious thought to make this end more sure by careful observance of sacrificial rites and customary duties, or even, in extreme cases, by ascetic practices of various kinds. But just before the rise of Buddhism there had been, due greatly to favorable political and economic conditions, a remarkable increase in the popularity of all sorts of theosophic speculation; and numerous teachers, not by any means always Brahmins, were posing as sophists, and as teachers of new things.

Under two such teachers the future Buddha at first, immediately after his renunciation, studied. But, being dissatisfied with their teaching, because it dealt more with the attainment of self-induced trance than with the ethical training he desired, he left them, to work out the question by and for himself. We cannot, therefore, be surprised to find, either, on the one hand, that the system he afterwards put forth bore evident traces of the previous speculation, or, on the other, that it differed so greatly from that speculation in matters fundamental that it stamps him as the most original of all the leading religious teachers of the world.

His system aims, like the previous ones, at salvation from transmigration. But he went behind transmigration. Why did they all dread this endless transmigration unless renewed becomings meant also renewed sorrow? The object to be aimed at must, therefore, be, above all and after all, the conquest of sorrow. But what is sorrow other than a subjective feeling, an experience of one's own mind? It is the separation from the loved and liked, the enforced union with the dreaded and disliked, the sense of wants unsatisfied, the sense of growing old, of decay and death. Now, all these are found wherever a separate individuality is found. And that is the reason why these constant becomings, these reiterated rebirths (which always involve a separate individuality) are bound up with sorrow.

What brings all this about? It is the unsatisfied longings at the moment of death that cause the rebirth. (Here the Indian thinker agrees, not only with his own predecessors, but also with Plato.) And these longings are, always and only, of three kinds—the lust of the flesh, the lust of life, and the love of this present world. To lay these, then, aside, to get rid of them, to become free from them—that would be the means to the end that all the religious thinkers of that day equally desired.

But these ignoble longings are also things of the mind, the outcome of a man's own heart. The way, then, and the only way, to the conquest of them must be the conquest of one's own heart by the cultivation of the opposite dispositions. No theosophical speculation, no views about one's soul, no hopes of a future life, no sacrifices, no penances, no external aid, can here avail. Nay, more than this—reliance on one or all of these expedients only serves to turn the attention away from the only useful struggle, which is the struggle after self-conquest. The other, then so popular, methods are all worse than useless, they are actually pernicious.

Now, self-conquest is not so easy. It must be carried on gradually, and according to a system, or the intellectual and ethical effort will be vain. The system put forward by the Buddha is well known as the Noble Eightfold Path (in Pali the Ariyo Aṭṭhangiko Maggo), that is to say:

1. Right Views.
2. Right Aspirations.
3. Right Speech.
4. Right Conduct.
5. Right Livelihood.
6. Right Effort.
7. Right Mindfulness.
8. Right Rapture.

To have reached the end of this eight-fold path, to have made each of its eight divisions part and parcel of one's own nature, to have *become* all that it implies, is Arahatship or Nirvana. And the unshakable emancipation of heart which the Arahat then enjoys is described as the aim and the essence, the pith and the goal, of Buddhism.[1]

How tame it must have seemed, how empty, how pale, compared with the sacrificial rites, or the elaborate penances, or the high-flown theosophies of the other religious teachers! One can almost hear the sneer of the worldly-wise superior person of that day against the "platitudes of the Noble Eightfold Path;" one can almost feel the want for something more supernatural, more striking, that would at once be felt by the theosophists on hearing the simplicity of this new doctrine.

Whether one agrees with Buddhism or not, it is easy to see that these objections, at least, are unfounded, exaggerated. It may be a platitude that every man ought to have right views. It is not a platitude—most men would deny

---

[1] Majjhima, I., 205.

it (and none more contemptuously than the superior person)—that every man ought to have right rapture. It was not only not a platitude, it was either a colossal blunder or a new truth of the very greatest weight, that salvation was to be sought in a state of mind, and in that only. Whether right or wrong, no one in the history of the world had hitherto put forward such a doctrine. And it certainly was not a simple matter that these eight, and just these eight, should have been held to be, in themselves, sufficient. Nor was it so simple even to grasp what the eight points, thus deliberately chosen, actually did, and did not, include and mean; still less what the Path, as a whole, leads up to and involves. Whatever else it was, early Buddhism was a most original, a most carefully thought out and balanced system.

This system is explained in the collection of 186 Dialogues of the Buddha preserved to us in the Buddhist sacred books. The forty-third of these Dialogues is devoted to the elucidation of what is meant by right views. It will be well, even only as a specimen, to set out in detail what this elucidation is as explained in the ninth of the Dialogues of lesser length. And, first, the man of right views understands what is evil and what is good, and the roots of each. And, again, he knows what are the four bases of bodily and mental life, and how these bases come into action and afterwards cease. The four, it may be mentioned in passing, are food, contact (through the senses with the outside world), mental activity, and consciousness. There is no mention either of Brahmā or of a soul or of intuitive ideas. As a consequence of this knowledge, the disciple gets entirely rid of sensuality and of ill will toward other beings, for he roots out of his heart the tendency toward the pride that arises from the belief in an ego; and thus, conquering delusion and gaining wisdom, he, even while yet in this present world, makes an end of sorrow.

And, again, he knows what sorrow is, and its origin and its cessation—how it is bound up with the temporary individuality resulting from the evanescent union of the five groups of bodily and mental qualities (which go to make up each individual); how it results from craving, and ceases in Arahatship.

And, again, he knows what old age and death mean, the getting aged and broken and white and wrinkled, the approaching end of one's allotted span of life, the breaking up of one's bodily organs; and the fall out of the class of beings to which one belongs, the disintegration of the five groups, the vanishing away from the sphere that one has filled—how both of them, death and old age, come from birth, and how both are overcome by Arahatship.

And, again, he knows about birth and

becoming, and about the grasping and thirst from which they come, and how all of these cease in Arahatship.

And he knows about the sensations and about the ideas that follow thereon, how they arise and what they lead to; and about name, and form, and consciousness, and mental predispositions; how all have their root in ignorance, and how ignorance can be analyzed ultimately into the four great evils—lust and becoming, delusion, and unwisdom. When he knows all this, then is his insight right, his views are straight, and endowed with an abiding trust in the truth; he has entered into the realm of the good law.

It may safely be said that no one, if asked to define right views, would give precisely this explanation. We have here unfolded to us what was then, and what is still, a new and original view of the mystery of life. The "soul" theory, which lies at the basis of all other religious systems, is conspicuous only by its absence. And there is no reference to any final causes. There is, indeed, a constant reference to causes and effects—very often of a kind that must seem strange, and at first sight almost unintelligible. But the main thesis is that life is the result of a temporary collocation of conditions that are always changing and are constantly tending to dissolve. To be able to trace the rise of any one state from the immediately preceding one is part of "right views." To be able to explain the ultimate and necessary first cause, or causes, is no such part. It is implied (and is elsewhere explicitly stated) that to have views about ultimate questions is a positive danger, inasmuch as it leads the man who holds them to rest on them without paying that strict attention to the immediate causes that it is so important for him to grasp.

But the inevitable limits of space preclude any further comment on this statement of the right views that are the first thing necessary to the Noble Path. The right aspirations are explained in the twenty-ninth Dialogue. Lowest of all comes the aspiration after a sufficient livelihood, and the regard and respect of one's fellow-men. Better than this is the aspiration after rectitude of life. Better again than that is the aspiration after the rapture and the mental peace that arise from the insight of meditation. Still better is the aspiration after certainty of knowledge. And best of all is the aspiration after that emancipation of heart that, first obtained as a temporary, momentary state, may by continued effort be made a permanent part of one's very being. That is the thing—this unshakable emancipation of heart—which is the meaning, and the pith, and the end of the whole matter.[1]

---

[1] Taken in abstract from Majjhima I., pp. 192–197, where the reference is to members of the Order.

The interpretations of right speech and conduct and livelihood and effort are not so different from the ordinary meaning attached to similar expressions in the West. But they leave out everything not in harmony with the above. Right livelihood, it may be added, involves,. among other things, that it brings hurt or danger to no living thing —a far-reaching ethical proposition that, if rigidly observed, would play sad havoc with many modes of livelihood highly honored in the present social conditions of the West. Right effort has, of course, nothing to do with getting on and making money. It is a never-flagging activity of the mind directed to ethical ends. And the important place it occupies in the " Path " is in striking contradiction to the constant hints in popular literature at the apathy and the idle, dreamy sort of existence supposed to be characteristic of Buddhism.

Right mindfulness would be almost inevitably misunderstood by Western readers without the aid of commentary. It means a constant presence of mind in all the ordinary acts of life, never for one moment forgetful of the real facts of the subjective and objective phenomena that are ever passing before one's mental vision. This is set out in detail in many passages in the Sacred Books, and two of the Dialogues are devoted exclusively to it. There it is laid down that this constant mental alertness is the only method for purification, for getting beyond grief and woe, for putting an end to sorrow and suffering, for the realization of Nirvana.[1]

Finally, right rapture is the peace of heart which follows on the sense of victory gained; and is realized by that steadfast concentration of mind in which the sense of "This is I" and "This is

---

[1] See, for instance, Majjhima I., 55–63.

mine" has been finally got rid of and overcome.[1]

The system is pieced together like a puzzle. Each detail is only really mastered when its particular place in the system is kept before one's mind. An exposition confined to the necessarily narrow limits of such an article as the present one can attempt to deal with only the more fundamental and general features of the scheme. To any one who will study it, it is full of suggestion for practical application in the ethics of to-day. And its great value is the aid which it affords to the student of the comparative history of the development of human thought.[2]

---

[1] Compare Anguttara III., 32, with Milinda 325, and Samyutta IV., 297, 350, and Dhamma Sangani II, 15, 24.

[2] Further information will be found in my just published "American Lectures," and in the authorities there referred to.

III

CONFUCIANISM

BY THE REV. ARTHUR H. SMITH

Author of "Chinese Characteristics"

What is Confucianism? By Confucianism we mean the essential teaching of those works which the Chinese reckon as classics. According to the narrowest enumeration, these are five in number— the Book of Changes, the Book of Odes, the Book of History, the Book of Rites, and the Spring and Autumn Annals. To these are also added the Conversations of Confucius, the Book of Filial Piety, the Works of Mencius, and Rituals and Commentaries, making a total of thirteen. The aggregate bulk of these works is probably somewhat less than that of our Old Testament, but if the Commentaries are included the classics comprise in themselves a vast library.

Theoretical Confucianism is to be got at by a distillation of these ancient books, and the writer of this paper wishes to disclaim any special fitness for the task of discussing a topic so comprehensive and of which he knows so little at first hand.

At the Chicago Parliament of Religions by far the longest essay presented was by the Hon. Pung Kwang Yu, Secretary to the Chinese Legation at Washington. It extends to sixty-six pages, more than ten times the average length of the papers read there, and is an elaborate discussion of many branches of our subject. It is of special interest, "as it is the first exposition ever given of Confucianism in English by a distinguished and able man, himself a Confucianist. It is also the first attempt of such a man to estimate the relative value of all religions, especially of Christianity. In addition to this, it gives us the view which the Chinese Government holds of Christian missions to-day." The writer of that essay was asked not to make it "technical," but he found it impossible to make it otherwise. The writer of the present paper is requested to make it "popular," but this he feels more and more convinced to be impracticable as he considers the matter longer. To most readers the Confucian classics are inaccessible, but the report of the Parliament of Religions has been sown broadcast over the whole earth. It seems, therefore, best to summarize, as briefly as may be, the essential parts of Mr. Pung's exposition, and those who wish for further elucidation have only to study his essay for themselves. Economy of space forbids more than a mere abstract, but we shall endeavor to give the spirit of Mr. Pung's thoughts without at all following his order:

While it is not true, as some claim,

that China has no religion of her own, Confucianism is an ethical system, and is not a "religion" at all. Thousands of years ago the Chinese were obliged to give up religion as a basis of government, because when secular and spiritual matters were mixed, misfortunes and calamities befell the nation. Nothing could now induce the Chinese to consent that civil and religious affairs should intersect each other.

There is a Spirit who rules this universe of created things; who accomplishes all his purposes without effort; whose presence cannot be perceived by the senses; who dwells ever in an atmosphere of serene majesty; who is the dispenser of all things, eternal and unchangeable. Before the creation of the universe he existed, and after the dissolution of the universe he will remain the same. He is called "Ti," Supreme Ruler. "Ti" is synonymous with heaven, and there is only one such.

Heaven and earth constitute a dualism. The conjunction of their vital essences brings forth a third, the inscrutable part of which is called a spirit. Heaven unites its essences with those of the sun, moon, and stars, and spirits of heaven result. In a similar way the spirits of mountains, rivers, and seas are produced. When any of these spirits in some special way benefit creation, the national government canonizes them, and they then take their place by the side of heaven.

Man is the product of heaven and earth, the union of the active and passive principles, the conjunction of the soul and spirit, and the ethereal essence of the five elements. Being the connecting link between unities and dualisms, man is called the heart of heaven and earth. Spirit must not be confounded with nature. Nature is an active element, matter is a passive element. To the interaction of the essences of the active and the passive principles the spirits of mountains, marshes, birds, insects, and of man are due. The spirit of man is in a more concentrated and better disciplined state than the spirits of the rest of the created things. For this reason the spirit of man, after death, though separated from the body, is able to retain its essential virtues, and does not become easily dissipated. This is the ghost or disembodied spirit.

Spirits owe their existence to material substances, and as the substances may be useful or noxious, so spirits may be benevolent or malevolent. A man whose heart is good must have a good spirit. Spirits attract one another, and when good spirits attract one another, this is happiness. When bad spirits attract one another, this is misery. When the bad spirits produce misfortune and calamities, the wise legislator puts his reliance on music and ceremonies to adjust the social equilibrium. His aim is to restore the human heart to its pristine innocence by establishing a standard of goodness, and by pointing out a way of salvation to every creature. The right principles of action can be discovered only by studying the waxing of the active and passive elements as set forth in the Book of Changes, and surely cannot be understood by those who believe in what priests call the dispensations of Providence. Man is endowed with faculties of the highest dignity, but if men lose this dignity in unlimited indulgence, even heaven cannot possibly do anything for them; but if, after experiencing a sense of shame mingled with fear and trembling, they repent of their evil doings, they become men again with their humanity restored. This is a doctrine maintained by all schools of Confucianists.

Nature is grand and impartial in its actions. The rule of life should be conformity to nature. To devote one's attention to the investigation of the laws of the spiritual world is unprofitable. Consequently Confucius made man his study, and would not discourse on wonders, brute force, rebellion, and spirits. He says that the art of rendering effective service to the people consists in keeping aloof from the spirits as well as in holding them in respect. "We have not yet performed our duties to men," he says; "how can we perform our duties to spirits?" "We know not as yet about life; how can we know about death?" "He who has sinned against Heaven has no place to pray." Under such circumstances any attempt to present before the people questions and problems that are incomprehensible and incapable of demonstration serves only to delude them by a crowd of misleading lights and to lead them to error and confusion. The wise rulers of antiquity laid down rules of propriety for the regulation of the three "superior claims," to wit, that of the sovereign, the father, and the husband, as well as of the "five relations," namely, those of sovereign and subject, of parents and children, of husbands and wives, of elder and younger brothers, and of friends toward one another.

All intelligent Chinese have for this reason been followers of Confucius, and Confucius really succeeded to the ancient line of priests. To do reverence to spirits is to do nothing more than to refrain from giving them annoyance, and to do reverence to Heaven is nothing more than to refrain from giving it annoyance. On these points the ritual code is explicit, and there is, therefore, no demand for other religious works. What is properly called religion has never been considered as a desirable thing for the people to know and for the government to sanction. The reason is that every attempt to propagate religious doctrines in China has always given rise to the spreading of falsehoods and errors, and finally resulted in rebellions and dire calamity. It makes not the least difference whether the particular form of religion teaches truth or error, nor what the character of the propagandists may be. The final result is ever the same, except that a religion that teaches error precipitates a crisis more speedily, that is all.

Both Taoists and Buddhists teach of future rewards and punishments. The purpose in doing so is laudable; it is the perpetuation of falsehood by clinging to errors that deserves condemnation. Confucianists do not accept such doctrines, though they make no attempt to suppress them. Heaven and hell are found in this life, without troubling the Buddhist Pluto and the Christ of the Christians to judge the dead after death, and reward every man according to his deserts. As a rule, men given to speculations on the world of spirits are forgetful of the duties of this life, and while employed by officials on occasions of public worship, they are at the same time despised by the Confucianists as the dregs of the people. As Buddhism says nothing of the regulation of the family, the government of the State, and the pacification of the world, there can be no conflict between Buddhism and the affairs of state.

There are many resemblances between the teachings of Christ and those of Confucianists, but the New Testament is very meagre on questions respecting the human faculties and the principles of morality, while the Confucian writers are very full. There is a Trinity in Taoism, a Trinity in Buddhism, and a Trinity in Christianity. If, by living according to the dictates of nature and by suppressing the desires of the flesh, one arrives at perfect agreement with nature, and obtains a complete mastery over desires, such a one Buddhists call a Buddha,

Taoists a genius, and Christians a child of God. It is idle for thinkers to attack one another, for all men cannot possibly arrive at the same opinion on any subject. The progress of Christianity does not concern Confucianists in the least.

Thus far the Hon. Pung Kwang Yu. To this ought to be appended a quotation from a speech of Li Hung Chang in New York last autumn, in which he said to a delegation representing missionary interests: "In a philosophical point of view, as far as I have been able to appreciate, Christianity does not differ much from Confucianism, as the Golden Rule is expressed in a positive form in one, while it is expressed in the negative form in the other. It is at present enough to conclude that there exists not much difference between the wise sayings of the two greatest teachers, on the foundations of which the whole structure of the two systems of morality is built."

There are six essential elements of Confucianism, five of which, so far as we know, differentiate it from any other system of non-Christian thought. Of these, the first is its doctrine of *the direct responsibility of the sovereign to Heaven, Shang Ti, or God.* This is abundantly illustrated in the classical writings, and it is a factor of the government of the present day as really as in times past. From this source originates the whole complex theory of Chinese responsibility, which plays so large a part in the conduct of all Chinese affairs, private as well as public. Only the Emperor worships Shang Ti, although the people do reverence to "heaven and earth," with very little conception of what it is that they worship.

The second element is the startling theory that *the people are of more importance than the sovereign.* The latter reigns by the decree of Heaven. When he loses Heaven's decree, he has no longer, the right to rule. The Chinese theory of government has been compendiously described as despotism tempered by the right of rebellion—a right constantly exercised in every period of Chinese history. This feature of Chinese rule makes it the most unique combination of absolute monarchy and "triumphant democracy" that the world has ever seen.

The third element is *the clear recognition of the various social relations*, as already described. To a Chinese these five relations exhaust the universe, just as a Christian considers the Ten Commandments to be co-extensive with human activity. As a matter of fact, it is easy to show that many "relations," such as those between capital and labor, for example, find no recognition at all.

The fourth element is *the lofty moral system of Confucianism*. The five constant virtues are benevolence, righteousness, propriety, knowledge, and good faith. The virtues are far oftener talked of in China than the precepts of the New Testament in Christian lands. They form a standard which is brought to the attention of all Chinese continuously. The civil service examinations, a slow growth of many ages, have unified the Chinese mind as the mind of no other people was ever unified, unless the Jews form an exception. The Chinese habit of using sententious classical mottoes for the adornment of their door-posts, mottoes written afresh at every New Year season, keeps the Confucian maxims always before the eye of the whole Chinese race. They are employed with varied iteration in all primary text-books, and the classics themselves form the sole and sufficient staple of all Chinese learning. It is an integral part of the theory that only the wise and the able should rule. The object of the elaborate civil service examinations is to determine who the wise and the able are.

The fifth element is *the presentation of an ideal or princely man* as the model on which every Confucianist should form his character. The influence of this ideal upon the unnumbered millions of Chinese Confucianists must have been measureless. Confucius enounced the Golden Rule in a negative form, but he affirms in the same connection that he himself had not attained to it. This places before all followers of the sage the ambition to live up to the high level which the master himself had not reached. Self-examination is inculcated by the precepts and by the example of the greatest rulers and wise men of antiquity. No nation, no race, was ever better outfitted with admirable moral precepts than the Chinese.

The last element of the six, only less distinctly Chinese than the others, is *filial piety*. This includes not only that meaning naturally suggested to Orientals, but a great deal more, and in especial the worship of ancestors, which is the real religion of the Chinese people. It is perhaps the most potent among several causes which have perpetuated the Chinese race as a unit through all the millenniums of its vast history. It is itself an illustration of the saying of an emperor of a famous dynasty more than a thousand years ago, that Confucianism is adapted to the Chinese people as water to the fish.

To those who believe that all truth is in its origin one, there need be no hesitation in admitting that the sages who uttered the principles underlying the Confucian tenets were in a sense divinely illuminated. Theirs was not the inspiration which we find in the Christian Scriptures, but they saw clearly profound, far-reaching, and eternal truths.

Thus far we have spoken only of theoretical Confucianism. It is of importance to remember that Confucius was in no sense the founder of the system which goes by his name. He himself declared that he was not an originator, but a transmitter. It was his glory to have caught all the rays of light coming from the dim past, and to combine them into one torch which has ever since lit up the Chinese path. But there was a Confucianism before Confucius; Taoism, or Rationalism, which has been its sole native rival, has to some extent modified Confucianism by interaction. Taoism taught the art of reducing nature by processes analogous to European alchemy, and the possibility of an elixir of life, thus attaining immortality. Yet this must always be the reward of the few. Buddhism, invited to China by an emperor more than six hundred years after the birth of Confucius, attempted to fill the void in the human heart which longs for salvation and for a saviour. The success of this misty and chameleon faith among the millions of hard-headed, practical

Chinese has been phenomenal. For ages Confucianism was its bitter foe, but as a matter of fact these three discordant contradictories have been interblended in a way perhaps elsewhere unexampled on this earth. Temples are found all over the empire in which the founders of the "three religions" stand side by side, and by perpetual repercussion for several hundred years the maxim that the three doctrines are one has come to be almost as much believed as the doctrines themselves. The same circumstance has resulted in such a complex of faith, in three sets of tenets which are, in Hamiltonian phrase, "incompossible," as to confound those Occidental statisticians who insist upon supposing that every man must either believe something or believe something else; whereas a Chinese believes, or supposes that he believes, something *and* something else.

The reader who has followed the fore going abstract of the most recent exposition of Confucian doctrine is prepared to judge in how many essential particulars it fails to give light. Its Shang Ti is remote and out of relation with mankind. He is not a Father, and the people are not allowed to worship him. Prayer is a ceremony by which evils are avoided and blessings insured. Polytheism is not only sanctioned, but necessitated. There is no explanation of sin and no remedy for it. For those to whom the ideal is inaccessible there is no salvation. Mere example is elevated into a force sufficient to keep the race on the right path. There is no explanation of its failure to do so, and no remedy for the failure. Ancestral worship is equivalent to the enlargement of the Chinese Pantheon to include all dead parents. This rite takes precedence of all others, and leads to the indefinite and reckless propagation of millions of persons for whose support there is no adequate provision. To this end polygamy, with all its immeasurable woes, is a practical necessity. Confucianism subordinates the children to the parents as long as the parents live, and prevents the normal development of those thus conditioned. The highest result of an ideal Confucian life is a cold formalism, and its inevitable tendency is to foster exaggerated self-esteem. It has resulted in the practical deification of its leading sages, but no one has any hope of reproducing their example in practice. It is a current saying that there are but two ideal men—one is dead, the other not yet born! This aphorism aptly voices the hopelessness of Confucianism.

Judging from a background of twenty-five years' acquaintance with China, one may pass through four distinct stages in his estimate of Confucianism. Coming to it from the atmosphere of a study of comparative religion, he is prepared to find it the best system ever devised by the mind of man for solving the problems of the race. He reveres the sages, and is anxious to conserve all that is good in their teaching. After some years of experience he becomes alive to the cavernous depths of sorrow and misery for which Confucianism has no help and no sympathy. The hollowness of its high-sounding but empty verbiage grates upon the ear, and he is weary of suspicion and insincerity masquerading in the garments of antiquity.

By this time a renewed observation of the actual state of the Occidental world serves to restore the balance of judgment. He there beholds many evils which are not forced to the front in China, and he recognizes the fact that there is no such unity of thought in any Western land in regard to ideals as there is in China. After a prolonged contemplation of the restless world at large, he returns to China full of generous hopefulness that his former opinions may have been overdrawn. But a reëxamination of all the phenomena which he sees, a reperusal of the data upon which previous judgments were formed, inevitably lead to a more emphatic reaffirmation of the proposition that Confucianism is a spent force. Its golden age is in the past, while the outlook of every Christian land is toward the morning dawn of a bright future. After listening to the varied eloquence of the speakers at the Parliament of Religions, one is compelled to ask, What, after all, is the essential difference between the Orient and the Occident? We believe it to be this: In the former, when things are as bad as they can be, they get worse; in the Occident they slowly tend to an improvement. Confucianism has within it no further energy for the evolution of good, but it is a powerful conserving influence. China is in a far sounder condition morally than was the Roman Empire in the time of Christ. We believe that China is sounder morally than Mohammedan Turkey, or than polyglot, metaphysical India. But, great as has been its work, Confucianism is inert. It is dead. Sooner or later it must give way to something stronger, wiser, and better.

IV

MOHAMMEDANISM

By the Rev. George Washburn, D.D.
President of Robert College, Constantinople

Mohammedanism is a positive religion based upon the Koran and the life and teaching of Mohammed. The Koran is believed to be literally the word of God, communicated directly to the Prophet, and written at his dictation. It is inspired not only verbally but in punctuation, and although the original writings were destroyed, there is every reason to believe that we have it in essentially the same form in which Mohammed left it. All Moslems accept it and use it, believing that the divine words have a mystic power whether they are understood or not. If translated, it is no longer the word of God.

But it is the life and teaching of the Prophet as set forth by the Imams, rather than the Koran, which is the practical basis of Mohammedanism, and controls the faith and life of the people. Every effort was made during the lifetime of those who personally knew the Prophet to collect and record all the incidents of his life and all his sayings. These were carefully sifted, and formed the basis of several lives of the Prophet, and of collections of traditions in regard to him, graded, according to the weight of testimony, into several classes. The division of his followers into Sunnis and Shiahs, and of these into a multitude of contending sects, grew out of the question of the succession to the Caliphat, and of the interpretation of these traditions. Most of the Sunnis are followers of the Imam Hanifa, who was born at Kufa, and lived from 80 to 150 A.H. He was the great theologian of Islam. He based his teaching upon the Koran, the traditions of the sayings and acts of the Prophet, the sayings and acts of the earlier Caliphs, and logical deductions from all these. It is a most elaborate system of philosophy, theology, and law, and is the chief study of the Ulema to this day. There are rival systems by the Imams Shafei, Malek, and Hanbal, but they have few followers. It is impossible to enter here upon any discussion of these systems or even an enumeration of the hundreds of Mohammedan sects, but it is necessary to remember that, whatever one may think of the Koran, it plays about the same part in Islam as that of the Old Testament in modern Judaism. It is the sacred book, but not the source of either the beliefs or the morals, of the people.

In deciding what is essential to a religion it is always desirable to have the testimony of some one who professes it, and is an authority recognized by his co-religionists. In this case we have an official letter, written ten years ago, by the Sheik-ul-Islam, the highest authority possible, to a German gentleman who had written to him for information as to how he could become a Moslem. I quote all the essential parts of this statement:

> The religion of Islam has for its basis faith in the unity of God and the mission of the Prophet. If you declare that there is one God and that Mohammed is his prophet, you are a Mussulman and our brother, for all true believers are brethren.
>
> This is a summary definition of faith. Now let us enter into its development. Man, who is superior to the other animals by his intelligence, has been created out of nothing to adore his Creator. This adoration consists in honoring the commands of God and in sympathizing with his creatures.

To enlighten men God has sent the prophets and the holy Koran. The greatest of all the prophets was Mohammed.

All the prophets threaten their followers with a Day of Judgment. So it is necessary to believe that the dead will rise, that they will appear before the tribunal of God to give an account, that the elect will be sent to paradise and the damned to hell. All the acts of soldiers in a holy war will be considered as prayer, and the martyrs will go to paradise without any examination into their lives.

Moreover, it is necessary to accept as an article of faith that God is the author of both good and evil. Consequently the believer ought to have faith in God, in his angels, in his books, in his prophets, in the last judgment, and to attribute both good and evil to the Divine Will. He who professes these verities is a *true* believer, but to be a *perfect* believer it is necessary to pray to God and to avoid falling into such sins as assassination, robbery, adultery, and sodomy.

In addition to the profession of faith a *good* Moslem ought to pray five times a day, to give away each year one-fortieth part of his goods, to fast during the month of Ramazan, and at least once in his life to make the pilgrimage to Mecca.

If a believer does not conform to these orders of God, and does not avoid what He forbids, he does not for this become an unbeliever. He will be considered as a sinner, that is to say, as a believer who has gone astray, and merits, in another world, a provisional punishment. He is at the disposition of God, who will pardon him or condemn him to pass a certain period in hell, proportioned to his guilt.

But faith annuls all sin. He who accepts Islamism becomes as innocent as a new-born babe, and is responsible only for the sins committed after his conversion. A sinner who repents, and who solicits in person the remission of his sins, obtains the divine pardon. The only exception is when we have violated the rights of our neighbor; for the servant of God who cannot obtain justice in this world will demand it at the last judgment, and God will accord it. To avoid this responsibility we must obtain an acquittance from the person wronged before we die.

There are no priests, no clergy, no mediators between God and man, in the faith of Islam. Only the religious ceremonies are subordinate to the will of the Caliph and Sultan, and " obedience to his orders is one of the most important of religious duties."

One of the things to which every Moslem

ought to be very attentive is integrity of character. Such vices as pride, presumption, egotism, and severity do not befit a Moslem. To revere the great and to compassionate the small are precepts of Islam.

Any one who will compare this plain official statement with the glowing pages of Syed Ameer Aali's "Life and Teaching of Mohammed" will realize how difficult it is for a student only of books to form a correct conception of what Mohammedanism really is; for no one doubts that Ameer Aali's book is perfectly honest, and that he conceives it possible to realize his conception of Islam; but, unfortunately, he represents only a small sect, and reaches his conclusions by ignoring most of what is recorded of the Prophet in the lives and traditions which other Mohammedans receive. He himself recognizes the fact that existing Mohammedanism does not at all resemble his ideal, either in theory or practice (page 284).

That Mohammed was an inspired prophet of God all his followers agree, though some deny that there was anything supernatural in his inspiration and arbitrarily reject most of the traditions. Nearly all, however, go to the other extreme—make him the first created spirit and his life miraculous from the dawn of creation to the present day. The question what his life and character really were is a study by itself, and we cannot enter upon it here. The life and character which determine the nature of Mohammedanism are those which appear in the traditions and in the earlier biographies. While there is a bright side to them and they exhibit many noble qualities, they are not conformed to Christian ideas of morality, and there are chapters, even in the Koran, referring to acts which could be excused to his own people only by a revelation from God. But there is nothing anywhere to justify the conclusion that Mohammed himself doubted the reality of his mission as a prophet called to preach the being and unity of God. That he believed this truth himself, that he was even ready to die for it, and that he held it to the end, I have no doubt. And this is the central thought of Mohammedanism—the one uppermost in the minds of all Moslems—that there is one Eternal, Almighty, Omnipresent, Personal God, who is the special friend and protector of all true believers. God is in all their thoughts. He is everywhere and in everything. Whatever is done, he does it. Whatever is known, he knows it. There is no limit to his wisdom or power. There is no perfection which he does not possess. He has ninety-nine names, each representing some divine attribute, but the one most often used is *the All-Merciful.* To those who confess his being and unity and recognize Mohammed as his prophet, he is always long-suffering and merciful.

To all others he is a consuming fire from which there is no possible escape in this world or the next. He is their implacable enemy.

The character of any religion may be tested by its conception of God and its teaching as to the nature of man. In this second respect also, Mohammedanism seems, at first sight, to be at one with Christianity. It teaches that man is a sinner, weak, corrupt, and absolutely dependent upon God's mercy for salvation. With these two great truths the Mohammedan mystic sometimes rises to the highest and most spiritual conceptions of God, and aspires to a life swallowed up in him. But if we examine these doctrines more closely, we find that the orthodox and common belief, based upon the life and traditions of the Prophet, gives us a very different conception of both God and man from that found in the New Testament. The God of Mohammedanism is an ideal Oriental despot magnified to infinity. The conception is not wanting in grandeur. All that Arabic poetry could do to exalt him has been done. Every perfection which it could conceive was attributed to him. Still he is an absolute Oriental monarch—all-powerful, all-wise, all-merciful towards his loyal subjects, but wreaking vengeance on all his adversaries—above all law, and infinitely removed from even the highest of his officials. Whatever he does or commands is right because he wills it. What he hates is not sin, but rebellion. He may or may not punish other offences, for he is all-merciful, but to deny his unity or his prophet is unpardonable. For this there is nothing but eternal fire. As there is no right or wrong except as he wills it, there is no true sense in which he can be called holy. Nor can it be said that he loves righteousness. What he loves is submission to his will, and this is the highest virtue known to Mohammedanism. It is what gives it its name—*Islam*, which means submission. Between God and man there is no kinship, nothing in common. He is not our Father and we are not his children. To use this expression as Christians do is blasphemy. If we are true believers, we are his sheep; if not, we are wolves. Consequently the idea of the incarnation of God in Jesus Christ is not only blasphemous, but absurd and incomprehensible. Whatever the Christian knows of God through the Incarnation is unknown to the Moslem.

The Mohammedan conception of the nature of man is fatalistic. It does not push fatalism to its logical conclusion and deny the reality of sin. The Prophet speaks of himself as a sinner dependent on divine mercy, although this is explained away by his followers as only a figure of speech. But while sin, punishment, and the pains of hell occupy a large place in the Koran and the traditions, while so much is said of the need of divine mercy, still the Moslem psychology is fatalistic, and the people look upon sin rather as a misfortune than a crime. The Moslem makes no distinction between the sensibilities and the will, and does not admit that he can resist or control his desires. He may avoid temptation, but he cannot resist it. God has made him weak, and hung his fate upon his neck. What can he do? If God has made him a Christian, Jew, or idolater, he will go to hell forever, however he may live in this world. This is his fate. If he is a Moslem, he will ultimately go to paradise, whatever his character. It is God's will. For one born a Moslem there is no place for conversion or regeneration. Man has no will to be changed. There is no such thing as an eternal principle of right. There is only the arbitrary will of God. Sin is disregard of God's law. He may punish it or not as he pleases. The idea that sin can corrupt and destroy the soul of a Moslem, or that character is fixed forever by our own act, is absurd. It is not salvation from sin that a man needs, but salvation from punishment. This depends on the will of God. As there is no necessity for regeneration, so there is none for an atonement, though the Moslem makes much of the advocacy of the Prophet. Christ was a great prophet, but in no sense the Saviour or Redeemer of the world. He did not die for the world, for the very good reason that he did not die at all, but was taken up to heaven, while one like him was crucified. When a Moslem feels the burden of sin, he feels it as a debt, and asks himself what good work he can do to offset it, or comforts himself with the thought that the Great King is too rich and merciful to press a poor, weak, but loyal subject for payment.

These brief statements are sufficient to show that the Moslem conception of man is the natural complement of its conception of God. While not absolutely fatalistic, it regards sin as a natural weakness, and character as a matter of fate rather than the effect of the choice of good or evil. Taken together, these two conceptions embody what is essential in the orthodox faith of Islam, and they are doctrines easy to be propagated, especially when championed by a conquering race. It does not require much mental effort to comprehend them, and their acceptance does not necessitate any change of character; while, at the same time, everything is promised to the convert which the soul demands—perfect immunity for all past sin, the special favor and protection of an omnipotent God and whatever man can desire in another world, while his instinct for worship is satisfied by an elaborate ceremonial code.

The ethical code of Islam is essentially that of the Old Testament, modified in some respects by the traditions of the life of the Prophet and by the philosophy of Hanifa and the other Imams. In practice it is also modified by the Moslem conception of the nature of man and by the fact that the ideal man of Islam is Mohammed. Whatever he is supposed to have done or approved is worthy of imitation. It is also peculiar in that it makes a broad distinction between the duties which Moslems owe to each other and those which they owe to unbelievers. As the Moslem rejects the fatherhood of God, so he denies the brotherhood of man. All true believers are brethren; all others are dogs. If they quietly submit to Moslem rule, pay tribute, make themselves useful, and are good dogs, they are to be tolerated and treated with kindness; otherwise the men are to be killed and the women and children sold as slaves (Koran, Sura IX.). This distinction is elaborated in the works of Hanifa, which are the principal study of the Softas. There are, of course, many Moslems, like Ameer Aali, whose relations with Christians are such that they have no sympathy with this orthodox view.

The working of this principle has been illustrated by the plunder and massacre of the Armenians during the past two years in Turkey. It has been done in the name of the Prophet, with the sanction of the Caliph, by the hands of Moslems, who have gone from the mosque to the massacre believing that they were doing God's will. At the same time a large number of Turks have condemned the massacres, and have done all that they could to defend the lives of the Armenians. Tens of thousands of Armenian lives have been saved in this way, and some distinguished Ulema have declared that neither the massacres nor the forced conversions could be justified. This difference does not arise from any doubt as to the principle involved, but from a question of fact. If the whole Armenian nation is to be considered in a state of rebellion against the Caliph, then all that has been done has been strictly in accord with the teaching of Islam. I have met no Turk who held any other opinion. But if only a few individuals have been in rebellion, then there is no justification for the plunder and slaughter of thousands of innocent and submissive people, even if they were unbelievers. It is on this ground that they have, in many cases, been protected by pious Moslems.

The specific duties which a perfect Mussulman owes to God and his brethren, and the special sins which he is to avoid, are stated in the letter of the Sheik-ul-Islam. The duties are prayer, alms, fasting, pilgrimage, and, in case of need, holy war; in general to obey the commands of God and compassionate his creatures, to revere the great and pity the weak. He should avoid such sins as assassination, robbery, adultery, sodomy, pride, presumption, egotism, and harshness. The Koran says: "God promises his mercy and a brilliant recompense to those who add good works to their faith." Omer Nessefi says: "It is an indispensable obligation for every Moslem to practise virtue and avoid vice, *i.e.*, all that is contrary to religion, law, humanity, good manners, and the duties of society. He ought especially to guard against deception, lying, slander, and abuse of his neighbor." In practice there are certainly many Moslems who try to observe these precepts, who fear God, and in their dealings with men, even with unbelievers, are honest, truthful, and benevolent, who are temperate in the gratification of their desires, and cultivate a self-denying spirit, of whose sincere desire to do right there can be no doubt. But the average Moslem, within my observation, is much more concerned with the formal than the spiritual side of his religion. This is also the testimony of Ameer Aali. He says, "The Moslems of the present day have made themselves the slaves of opportunism and outward observance."

Volumes have been written on points in Mohammedanism which I have not touched, but which undoubtedly make up the greater part of the life and thought of the majority of Moslems. The speculative theology and philosophy of Mohammedanism, though now somewhat antiquated in relation to modern thought, covers as wide a field as that of Thomas Aquinas, and is the basis of the teaching in the schools. The common people get their religious education from the lives and traditions of the Prophet, which are full of curious and fantastic legends of the times of the earlier prophets as well as of the delights of paradise and the sufferings of hell. The dervishes and their secret teaching are a study by themselves. Then there are great moral questions, such as slavery, polygamy, divorce, and holy war, which might be discussed at length. But my object has been to present only such points as all orthodox Moslems regard as essential to their faith, without controversy or any more of comment and explanation than seemed necessary to a right understanding of them.

V

BRAHMANISM

By Charles R. Lanman

Professor of Sanskrit, Harvard University

It is a cheering sign of the times that we are beginning to quit prejudice and are learning to look outward. We adopt a ballot-law from Australia simply because it makes for political righteousness; we waste no time to inquire, like Nathanael, "Can there any good thing come out of" that whilome limbo of deported convicts? And, now, at last, in religion, as well as in politics, we are ready to go to the ends of the earth, if so be we may find God's light and truth, and to take it at the hands of men whom we once scrupled not to call benighted heathen. "God, who at sundry times and in divers manners spake in time past unto the fathers by the prophets"—such is the splendid exordium of the Epistle to the Hebrews. To the Hebrews, "prophets" meant naught else than Hebrew prophets—small wonder. But to St. Paul—what would the meaning be to him, if we could question him about it to-day? He surely would be the last to limit it to the saints and sages of a "chosen people." Nay, rather, he would rejoice to find the accents of the Holy Ghost in Greece or even in India.

Brahmanism is exclusive rather than proselyting. It is not a world-religion; but we may not on that account deny that it has a message for the world. That message may consist on the one hand in truths which its doctrines include; or also, on the other, in lessons and warnings which modern thinkers of wider scope than any Hindu, may read from its long and often sad history.

The term Brahmanism is vague, and

forces us, even at the outset, to some prefatory definition. The Vedas are the sacred books of the Hindus, the oldest recorded documents of that branch of the human race to which we Anglo-Saxons belong. For our present purposes, the Vedas may be divided into three great strata: the Hymns, the Brahmanas, and the Upanishads. The Hymns (often called Veda in a narrower sense) are the oldest, and in them is reflected the simple nature-religion of a sturdy, life-loving people, the early Aryan Hindus. To them, the wind, the storm, the sun, the fire, the waters—each was the manifestation of a divine personality, of a god whose anger was to be appeased and whose favor was to be sought. The worship is on a give-and-take basis. The gods accept offerings of rice and butter, and bestow in return rain and food, children and cattle. Of lofty spiritual aspiration there is little in the Hymns of the old Vedic religion.

The simple rites of the fathers fell into the hands of a caste of priests whose interest it was to elaborate the rites into a system so complex that only they, the professional sacrificers, could perform them. The ancient nature-worship was transformed into a rigid, soul-deadening ritualism which is perhaps without a parallel. The sacrifice was apotheosized and invested with a supernal, a god-compelling power. This second great phase in the evolution of religions in India we name Brahmanism proper; the literature in which it is reflected we call the Brahmanas, and they seem to represent Indian thought at its lowest ebb. With it came a profound transformation of the Indian character. The life-loving strenuousness of the olden time has given place to pessimistic quietism. The belief in the transmigration of souls has become an established conviction, not of the learned only, but of the lowest and meanest.

We may liken the time to the hour of sultry stillness that precedes the storm.

For at this juncture, probably in the sixth century B.C., a new era of religious commotion began. Dreamers and mystics, reformers and saviours, seem to have arisen on all sides in Gangesland, full of new teachings, some lofty, some paltry, with which they were to reclaim men from the slough in which they were mired. Gotama Buddha was one of these teachers, the greatest and noblest personality of all Indian history. Another was Nigantha Nataputta, the founder, or rather the reformer, of Jainism. Still others of lesser note are named in the Buddhist Scriptures as propounders of various heresies. But next to Gotama, doubtless the greatest teachers of this time were the Brahman theosophists, men like Shandilya and Yajnavalkya, the authors of the doctrines of the Upanishads.

The Upanishads[1] teach the absolute identity of man and God, of the individual soul and the Supreme Spirit, and declare that only by recognition of its true nature can the soul be released from its attachment to the world-illusion, and from the consequent round of transmigrations. Ignorance is the root of all sin and evil. Salvation is by knowledge. And accordingly the Upanishads on the one hand form what the Hindus call the "Knowledge division" of the Vedas, as opposed to the old Hymns and Brahmanas on the other hand, which they call the "Work-division." The relation is like that of the New Testament to the Old—only that in India the antithesis is not between works and *faith*, but between works and *knowledge*. Since the Upanishads are held to

---

[1] The best work extant in any modern language of Europe upon the Upanishads is Paul Deussen's translation of them, with introductions, published lately by Brockhaus in Leipsic.

be the crown or capstone of all the Vedas, they are called Vedanta, literally, "the end of the Vedas." The doctrines of these theosophic treatises cannot be combined into one coherent philosophical system; they are too disconnected, contradictory, and disorderly. And the best proof of it is that several very diverse systems of philosophy were, as a matter of fact, built upon them. The Hindus admit six orthodox systems, the chief of which are the Vedanta system and the Sankhya system. Here are elaborated, with all the art and the technical skill of the Indian dialectician, the great rude thoughts of the Upanishads. To treat of the systems is beyond the scope of this brief paper.

Modern philosophical critics may admit or deny the value of the Upanishads and of the systems, as speculation; but the loftiness and honesty of purpose of these ancient teachers cannot be denied. They have never lost sight of the one great practical end of all their teaching, the liberation of the soul. As illustration may serve the final sentence of a famous Sankhya book. The author has just concluded a long argument, which, when turned from Sanskrit into the clearest English, is still surpassingly hard and knotty reading. Then follows his simple but impressive climax: "Be all my argument right, or be all my argument wrong, the ending of bondage to the world is the supreme aim of the soul."

The object of the Upanishads, then, is the search after God. The riddle of existence is scarcely broached in the oldest Veda. To the mystics of the Upanishads, the origination of the universe out of nothing is the question of questions; and if it proved as insoluble to them as to us, the grappling with it led at least to their one great contribution to human thought, the identity of the subject with the object, of man with

God, of the Atman with Brahman; in short, to the idealistic monism of the Vedanta system, and the supreme conception of the All-soul.

The word *atman* originally meant breath, and so the principle of life, the soul, the innermost self. A picturesque myth in one of the oldest Upanishads naïvely represents the Atman as a primeval being of human likeness, and all the creatures as proceeding from him by his creative act. Little as the gain from all this may be, it is yet the starting-point of the spiritual pantheism of India. It would be giving an epitome of Indian theology to explain the famous word *brahman*. At first it meant the power of devotion, of prayer, and especially of the sacrifice; and, finally, with the inordinate exaggeration of the sacrifice (as hinted above) into a power upon which even the gods were conceived as depending, Brahman came to be the power which is behind both the gods and the world, the eternal principle of all existence.

The acme of these doctrines is reached in the fusion of the originally subjective Atman with the objective Brahman into one supreme entity, transcending all limitations of space, time, and causality. The soul is not different from Brahm, because there is nothing existent outside of Brahm. The soul is not a transformation of Brahm, because Brahm is unchangeable. The soul is not a part of Brahm, because whatever has parts is transitory and suffers change, and Brahm, being unchangeable, can therefore have no parts. In short, then, the kernel of the whole doctrine is the direct immanency of God, an assumption unproved, and yet of profound practical import.

The central point of all this teaching is illustrated in a hundred ways, naïve and picturesque. We may cite one (Deussen thinks it the oldest) passage in which the doctrine is set forth. "Verily the universe is Brahm: whose substance is spirit; whose body is life; whose form is light; whose purpose is truth; whose essence is infinity. This is my spirit (or *atman*) within my heart, smaller than a grain of rice, or a barleycorn, or a grain of mustard-seed; smaller than a grain of millet, or even than a husked grain of millet. It is greater than the earth, greater than the sky, greater than the heaven, greater than all the worlds. The all-working, all-wishing, all-smelling, all-tasting one, that embraceth the universe, that is silent, untroubled—that is my spirit within my heart; that is Brahm. Thereunto, when I go hence, shall I attain. Thus spake Shandilya."

The chief end of man is salvation, that is, liberation from the bonds of death and rebirth, the endless rounds of transmigration. This liberation is effected, not by faith, but by knowledge, by the recognition of the absolute identity of my innermost being with God. What now is the way to this knowledge? For on it we must find the basis of the practical ethics of the Vedanta. The fallen state is the illusion of separation from God, and this illusion is fed by the desires and lusts of the world. Morality, therefore, is primarily rather negative than positive—the renunciation of the lust of the world, of wife, children, possessions, in short, of all the great activities of life.

So far as theories go, there is spiritual truth on both sides, for Christian and Hindu alike, to take and to give. To Hindu mysticism and to Christian mysticism alike are common the most grotesque fancies and the deepest truths; in both are elements which may prove to be of value for our religious life. It may be too that some of the Indian theories concerning personality when dissociated from Indian pessimism shall yet in these last days bear fruit. Did the Eastern mystic so lose himself in the beatific vision of God as to have little thought for his fellows? Possibly; but, *per contra*, are not we so feverishly asserting our individuality in all the details of life that we never quit the pin-fold in which we are confined and pestered? May not each of us learn from the other?

There is a Sanskrit work called the "Garland of Questions and Answers," in which some Hindu Nicodemus seeks to know what it is to be born of the Spirit. His question is:

What lack I yet? What for my soul remaineth
To know, that all these longings then may cease?

And the answer:

Salvation, wherein simplest soul attaineth
The knowledge that doth end in perfect peace.

And again:

What must I know, the which, when comprehending,
Their secret thought from all the worlds I wrest?

And the answer:

On all-embracing Brahm thy spirit bending,—
That know, Prime Form of Being, Manifest.

And we hustling Occidentals marvel and say, "How can these things be?" Mystical perhaps they are to our Western temper of mind; but are we quite sure that our temper is wholly right, and the only right one? In India as well as in Palestine was the warning given: "Except ye become as little children."

As for the Upanishads in practice, we little realize in the Occident how holy and saintly have been the lives of thousands of these quiet Vedantists. And even in characterizing renunciation as a negative virtue, there may be a touch of injustice and error. On the other hand, if we are right in our ideals of human progress, it is hard to see how they have been furthered by quietism. "I am come," said the greatest of teachers, "that they might have life, and that they might have it more abundantly." But even here again let me warn against over-confidence in the infallibility of the Occidental standards by which we would measure the fulness of life.

And it is well to remember here that —despite all the diversity of dogmas and of metaphysical conceptions, whether of Buddhism or Confucianism, whether of Christianity or the Vedanta—that the way of peace for all is by morality and not by immorality, that the ethical ideal is essentially the same the world over, that virtue is everywhere lovely, or, in mystic phrase, that she can quicken our spiritual sense until we catch the unheard music of the spheres.

> She can teach ye how to climb
> Higher than the sphery chime.

A change of attitude towards non-Christian religions has undoubtedly begun within Christendom. It is a step in advance, clear and great. Among its immediate results there may indeed be much unintelligible dabbling in Buddhism and sundry other "isms" of the East, and the growth therefrom of an irreverent and weak and flabby eclecticism; but these are transient extravagances. The new habit of mind, if only it be informed with honesty and humility, is an essential preliminary to the best general religious progress. It is something which the leaders of religious life and thought should welcome as a glorious, an inspiring opportunity.

VI

CHRISTIANITY

By Lyman Abbott

The object of this series of articles is to point out what is distinctive in each one of the great religions of the world. What is thus distinctive in Christianity is Jesus Christ. Other religions are greater than their founders. Confucianism is greater than Confucius, Buddhism than Siddartha, Judaism than Moses, Mohammedanism than Mohammed. But Christ is greater than Christianity; the Founder is greater than the religion which he founded. Its accretions are corruptions; it might almost be said that its development is degeneracy. The Sermon on the Mount is greater than the greatest of the creeds; the Lord's Supper is sublimer in its simplicity than the High Mass in its elaboration; the message and ministry of the twelve, with the Master as their leader, are larger events in history than all the complicated ecclesiasticism of the Middle Ages, with its clerical orders and sub-orders.

I. In Christianity the principles of the religion are exemplified and the spirit of the religion is embodied in a Person. The whole duty of the Christian is summed up in the Master's command, "Follow me." The whole creed of the Christian is summed up in "Ye believe in God, believe also in me." Confucius gave precepts whose value is wholly independent of the man who gave them; Siddartha is a shadow cast upon the clouds—no one can tell how much it resembles any historical original; Moses is avowedly only the interpreter of a law whose divine authority derives no sanction from the human law-giver; Mohammed is a true prophet of monotheism, but no reader of these pages would wish to emulate his life. But Christ is a living Person, whose historical reality skepticism itself no longer doubts, whose authoritative declarations as a faithful and true witness add to the sum of human knowledge, and whose life and character are both greater and more luminous than any report of his precepts which his immediate followers have preserved for us. Are we perplexed as to the meaning of any of his directions? we have but to ask an interpretation of his life. "But I say unto you, Love your enemies." "If one smite thee on the one cheek, turn to him the other also." His own treatment of Judas Iscariot, his own endurance of shame and insult in the court of Caiaphas, make the enigma clear to us.

And not only clear; also possible. "'Love your enemies;' that is not human nature"—this protest dies away, half uttered, upon our lips when we see what this Man has done in attestation of the possibilities of human nature. Confucianism, Buddhism, Mosaism, all present splendid ideals of life; Christianity differs from them less in the ideals presented than in the transcendent fact that it presents them realized. The divine life is no longer a poet's dream or a prophet's ecstatic vision of some future celestial glory. The kingdom of God has come down to earth. The highest hope of the idealist is no longer an impossible hope; it is a realized fact in human history. Christ is the ideal. To be a Christian is to be Christlike; there is nothing higher; when, if ever, all humanity becomes Christlike, the kingdom of heaven will have come on earth; there is nothing beyond.

Thus Christianity is at once idealism and realism in religion combined. It commends nothing which it does not demonstrate possible. When Christ asks his followers, "Can ye drink of the cup that I drink of, and be baptized with the baptism I am baptized with?" inspired by his example, and still more by his persuasive personality, they reply, "We can;" and he responds, "Ye shall." It is this quality of realism in the religion of Christ—a religion presented by its Founder, not as an impossible ideal, but as a reality, not as a vision of a hoped-for future, but as the record of undoubted history—which constitutes the first distinguishing mark of Christianity. Confucianism, summoning its adherents to pay veneration to an idealized past, Buddhism, bidding its adherents dream of an unrealized future, keep their votaries unchanged from century to century. Christ, calling the Christian to an ideal which he has realized in his own life, responds to every failure and every consequent discouragement, "You can, for I have. What I have done you can do; what I am you can become."

The followers of Christ, thus inspired by an ideal realized in history, rise from every defeat with a new hope of victory in their hearts, and go forward from every victory inspired to attempt new achievement. When they have abolished slavery, they immediately combine to fit the enfranchised for industrial freedom. When they have abolished private war, they rest not, but gather their forces together to abolish international war. They are not discouraged in the first case because the negro population grows faster than the schools, nor in the second because imperial Europe, with fanatical conservatism, persists in retaining a militarism inherited from pagan Rome. Nor does the fact that they are a minority, even in the community which calls itself Christian, abate their courage; for they look back and see what One accomplished with but twelve followers, and one of them a traitor. It is true that there is industrial servitude in our workshops as well as in the fields of China, that there are prostitutes in Christian as well as in Hindu cities, social caste in democratic America as well as in Brahmanical India, the spirit of militarism in Christian Europe as well as in Mohammedan Turkey. But Christianity has abolished the worst forms of industrial servitude and is ameliorating such as remain; there are no consecrated prostitutes in Christendom; caste exists in spite of religion in the United States, because of religion in India; the spirit of the Cross, patiently if peacefully, opposes itself to that spirit of militarism which the Crescent inspires and glorifies.

What is true of Christianity as a social force is true of it also as an individual life. Its history is written in splendid lives. It is the record, not merely of great thoughts, but of greater deeds; it is not merely the vision of splendid ideals, but the history of achievement, marred indeed by many a failure and many a blemish, but more splendid than any mere ideal, because deeds are always more splendid than dreams. Christianity is not a history of ethical rules, theological doctrines, or ecclesiastical systems; it is a history of living men and women; not a picture of piety, but the biography of saints; not a picture of heroism, but a biography of heroes; not a picture of patience, but a biography of brave men and women bearing the world's burdens. It is not the history of Romanism and Lutheranism and Puritanism and Wesleyanism; it is the biography of Augustine, and William of Orange, and John Hampden, and the Methodist pioneers. No other religion has written its history in such achievements and such biographies. Christianity is an ideal realized in the one Christ, and therefore in process of realization in Christendom; a spirit incarnated in the one Man, and therefore in the process of becoming incarnated in Humanity.

II. This realism of religion, which is a distinctive characteristic of Christianity, is due to the new *power* which Christianity confers upon mankind, or, to speak more accurately, to the new revelation which it affords of an eternal power.

That Christianity claims to confer such new power upon man is evident from the most casual reading of the primitive documents. It is implied in the declaration of Christ defining his mission: "I have come that they might have life, and might have it more abundantly." It is affirmed by Paul in his definition of the Gospel as "the *power* of God unto salvation." It is even more explicitly declared by John: "To them gave he *power* to become the sons of God, even to them that believe on his name." But it is not only occasionally and incidentally claimed for Christianity by its first evangelists; it is the theme of their teaching. They are not the framers of a new code of rules for the regulation of conduct, nor the teachers of a new system of philosophy—though their successors in the ministry have often been one or the other; they are the heralds of a Person. To understand their message we must remember that Christianity came to the world as the consummation and fulfillment of a precedent religion. One characteristic of the Jewish religion was its forelooking character. From the promise to Eve that her seed should crush the serpent's head to the prophecy of the great Unknown Prophet of the Exile that the Suffering Servant of the Lord should redeem Israel out of all his troubles, the Jewish people were taught by their prophets to look forward to a Deliverer and a Deliverance which should bring the kingdom of God on the earth. Whatever interpretation we may now give to these promises, there is no question, as matter of history, that, in the first century of this era, the Jewish people were universally expecting the coming of a Messiah, an Anointed One, who would fulfill the expectation of Israel, and redeem the nation, if not the world, from its sorrows. The burden of the preaching of the Apostles is that the Messiah has come, and the Day of Deliverance is at hand. It is not necessary to load these pages with quotations or even with references. The Apostolic sermons reported in the Book of Acts are the earliest recorded examples of primitive preaching. The burden of these sermons is always the same, that the Messiah has come, and that the evidence of his Messiahship is his resurrection from the dead. The Epistles of Paul are probably the earliest writings of the primitive Church. The burden of these Epistles is always the same, that "the law of the Spirit of life in Christ Jesus hath made me free from the law of sin and death," so that "we are more than conquerors through him that loved us." If we turn to the teaching of Christ, we find the same characteristic. At the beginning of his ministry, in the synagogue at Nazareth, he reads from an ancient prophecy the promise of One to come who will proclaim glad tidings to the poor, will heal the broken-hearted, will proclaim deliverance to the captives and recovering of sight to the blind, and will lead forth into liberty those that are crushed by oppression; and he declares that he has come to fulfill this promise. At the close of his ministry, put under solemn judicial oath by the high priest, and asked if he is the Messiah, the Son of the Living God, he replies that he is, and seals this claim with the surrender of his life. Modern discovery has made it clear that the Fourth Gospel was written and published early in the second century, if not late in the first century, and it contains, in all probability, a report of Christ's life and mission furnished by the Beloved Disciple, if not actually written by him. But we are not left to the Fourth Gospel for evidence that Jesus claimed to be the Christ, the

Anointed One, the Saviour of the world. This claim is wrought into his teaching concerning himself as recorded in the Synoptic Gospels, into the Apostolic heralding of his Person as recorded in the Book of Acts, into the thought and life of the earliest churches as reflected in the letters of Paul. The post-Apostolic writings and the very inscriptions in the catacombs illustrate the same claim of primitive Christianity. The earliest symbol of the Christians, used by them apparently as a sort of secret sign or watchword, was a fish. This word fish is formed in the Greek of the five letters which for the English reader we may represent thus: I, Ch, Th, U, S. Each letter represents a word which we may represent in English characters thus: JESOUS, CHRISTOS, THEOU, UIOS, SOTER—that is, Jesus, Christ, of God the Son, Saviour. This faith in a Person who brought a new life into the world, a new power to men, an emancipation, an enfranchisement, a deliverance, was the creed of the early Church. However skeptical one may be concerning the truth of this faith, one cannot doubt that the faith existed, and was the secret of the Church's existence.

As little can it be doubted that the world sorely feels the need of such a power. Whatever opinion the skeptic may entertain concerning the eighth chapter of Romans, there are few skeptics who will doubt the seventh chapter. "To will is present with me; but how to perform that which is good I find not," is the experience of all men who possess noble ideals. It is only the hopelessly self-conceited man to whom this declaration is meaningless. Much is said of the Gospel as a revelation; but we do not so much need to have new truth revealed to us as new power conferred upon us. It is easier to see the right than to do the right as we see it. Our ideals may be, and often are, ignoble, but they are nobler than our lives. To transmute dreams into deeds is the perpetually unsolved problem of every noble nature. That Christianity has conferred on all its votaries the power which man so sorely needs no one will claim; but that it has conferred on them new moral power, endowing with life, transforming the character, and revealed in the conduct, is abundantly illustrated by its history: in individual transformations like those of Paul the persecutor into the Apostle, Augustine the roué into the saint, Loyola the soldier into the churchman, Luther the monk into the emancipator, Bunyan the tinker into the prophet, Gough the drunkard into the temperance reformer; on a large scale, in the transformation of pagan Rome into Christian Europe, and the Anglo-Saxon race from the freebooters and pirates of the eighth century into the pioneers of civilization in the nineteenth. It may, indeed, be said that the progress is very slow, since it has taken eighteen centuries to make out of paganism a social order so little Christianized as that of modern Europe. But it must be remembered that the present population of Europe has been under the influence of Christianity, not eighteen centuries, but one-third of a century. Progress is necessarily slow in a world in which every thirty-three years a new class comes into life to acquire afresh all its knowledge and all its virtue.

However slow that progress may have been, it is certain that Christianity is the only world-religion which is characterized by those transformations of individual character which we call conversion, or that transformation of national character which we call progress. We hear much of the progress of humanity; but historically it has been confined to Christendom; the nineteenth century is much glorified, but in China and India the nineteenth century does not differ from the first. Christianity appears to me to be the only world-religion which even claims ability to make such transformations of character, to confer on man power to realize his ideals, to convert his aspirations into achievement. Neither Confucianism, Judaism, nor Mohammedanism can be said even to offer to man an addition to his powers, a reinforcement of his spirit, and an emancipation from his bondage. Buddhism, it is true, does offer a deliverance; Buddha does claim to be a Deliverer from the perpetual disappointments of life. But, as Professor Palmer has recently so clearly pointed out, Buddhism prescribes as the secret of deliverance the death of desire, Christianity proffers the power to fulfill aspiration. The rest of the one is the rest of death, that of the other is the rest of triumphant life.

III. I have said that this power to realize ideals which Christianity confers upon its adherents is not really new, but only a new realization of a power which is eternal; but this is equally true of that increased endowment which knowledge confers in the physical realm. Electricity is not a new force now first created, but an old force now first discovered or revealed. As the nature of electricity is revealed to us it becomes a practical power in our hands to be employed by us. Thus revelation or discovery,[1] while it does not add to the powers in the universe, increases our capacity to use them. The powers in the universe remain unaltered, but our power is increased.

In the moral realm the greatest of all powers is that of a great personality—that which one masterful character exercises over another character. This is the power of the great orator, who sways an audience as he will, not by acquired arts of rhetoric or elocution—these are only

---

[1] Synonymous words : to discover is to uncover, to reveal is to unveil.

his instruments—but by the personal character which employs them and is communicated by them. It is this which makes him what we call—concealing our ignorance by the meaningless word—a magnetic speaker. This is the secret of the great musician. More than the flute-like voice of the singer, more than the trained fingers of the violinist or the pianist, is the man or woman who is interpreted by voice or instrument. If this character is wanting, we may admire the technique, but go away untouched, saying, "But he had no soul." This is the power of the great general—the Little Corporal seizing the flag at the bridge of Lodi, and by his mere presence converting his hesitating soldiers into an irresistible torrent of brave men; General Sheridan meeting his panic-stricken soldiers fleeing from the field in the Shenandoah Valley, calling to them, "Turn, boys, turn! we are going the other way," and, by the power of his infectious courage, converting their panic into an enthusiasm of courage, and the rout into a victory. This is the secret of the mother's power. She goes down in solemn joy to that door which swings both ways on its hinges, not knowing whether she will go out into the unknown, or out of the unknown a new life will come to her; she offers her life in that very hour in which she welcomes a new life to her keeping; all her motherhood is one lifelong offering, a transmission of her life to the child, whom she endows with courage, truth, purity, love, not by her skilled teaching, but by the impartation of herself; not by what she says, nor yet by what she does, but by what she is.

Christianity, recognizing this power of a great personality, brings to bear upon humanity the personality of God. It differs somewhat from other world-religions in the ideals of human life and character which it presents. Yet in the main these agree; for the aspirations of humanity are ever alike in their trend, though not in their clearness and purity. Christianity differs more from other world-religions in its doctrine of God. Confucianism deifies its ancestors, Buddhism deifies its dreams, Mohammedanism deifies its conscience and its self-will; Christianity alone deifies love. But the distinctive characteristic of Christianity lies, not in its ideals—that is, its laws; not in its conception of God—that is, in its theology; but in this, that it so brings God down to earth, so interprets him an Immanuel, a God with us, that it discovers or reveals to man this eternal but before unknown power, the power of a divine personality living among men, brooding them, and by direct personal influence transforming them. God's silent voice transcends the magnetism of all world-orators; his inspiring presence summons to a courage unparalleled on any field of battle; his brooding care is more life-giving than that of any mother.

This is, to us who follow Christ and believe in him, the meaning of the Incarnation. In vain our imagination endeavors to realize an "Infinite and Eternal Energy," or a "Power not ourselves that makes for righteousness." But in Christ we see God personified; brought within our vision; so dwelling among us that his personality touches ours and we answer to the contact. This is what we mean by the doctrine of the Holy Spirit. He dwells with us and is in us, his Spirit so mingling with our spirit that all our life is reinforced by his presence, and what before was impossible becomes easy. This is what we mean by atonement. He is at one with us and we are at one with him, so that his life flows into us and we live by him. This is what the Psalmist means when he says, "By my God I have run through a troop, and by my God I have leaped over a wall." This is what Paul means when he says, "I can do all things through him that strengtheneth me." This is what he means by saying that we are heirs of God and joint heirs with Jesus Christ. We inherit God himself, become partakers of the divine nature, like Christ are sons of God, our life is begotten of God and proceeds from him. This is what he means by saying that our righteousness is of God by faith; as the listener enters into sympathy with the orator, the soldier with the hero, the child with the mother, so we enter into sympathy with God—that is faith. As life passes from orator to audience, from hero to soldier, from mother to child, so it passes from God to the human soul—that is grace. And this faith which receives and this grace which gives find, possibly analogies, certainly no parallel, in any other world-religion.

To sum all up: the distinctive characteristic of Christianity is Christ; by Christ God is brought to earth, made visible, tangible, comprehensible to us;

by this contact the divine personality comes in touch with us, reinforces our spiritual nature, endows us with new power, inspires, recreates, transforms; thus empowered, we are able to translate our before impossible ideals into realities, our dreams into deeds, our aspirations into achievements.

www.ingramcontent.com/pod-product-compliance
Lightning Source LLC
Chambersburg PA
CBHW020110170426
43199CB00009B/474